Original title:
The Glade of Giggles

Copyright © 2025 Creative Arts Management OÜ
All rights reserved.

Author: Arabella Whitmore
ISBN HARDBACK: 978-1-80567-417-7
ISBN PAPERBACK: 978-1-80567-716-1

The Grinning Grove

In the forest where laughter dwells,
Trees wear hats and tell tall tales,
Squirrels dance with silly grins,
Chasing shadows, making spins.

Bumbles bounce on breezy days,
With crazy steps and funny ways,
Frogs in bow ties croak a tune,
While butterflies plot to make us swoon.

Beneath the sun, a merry jest,
A playful breeze, a funky fest,
Rabbits in coats jump high and low,
As daisies twirl in a giggly show.

Oh, how the giggles fill the air,
With every leap, there's joy to share,
In this place where smiles ignite,
Laughter echoes, pure delight.

Frothy Laughter Lane

Down the lane where silliness sways,
Frothy bubbles dance and play.
Pigeons wearing hats parade,
Tickling tales in sunlit shade.

Jesters juggle with great flair,
Squeaky toys are everywhere.
Laughter ripples through the air,
Joyful echoes, without a care.

Whimsy in the Wilderness

In the woods where giggles sprout,
Trees wear shorts, there's no doubt.
Squirrels sing their silly tunes,
While frogs play chess beneath the moons.

Pandas slip on rainbow slides,
Tumbling over nature's rides.
Every corner holds a jest,
Whimsy's hiding, never rests.

Sunlit Snickers

Under skies of cotton candy,
Chasing shadows, feeling dandy.
Butterflies in top hats whirl,
As giggling flowers twist and twirl.

Bouncing bunnies tell a tale,
Of knickers worn by a happy snail.
Sunlit snickers fill the air,
With playful prances everywhere.

Joy's Enchanted Glen

In a glen where chuckles bloom,
Elves in pajamas loom.
Candy canes sprout from the ground,
While shy trolls hum their sound.

Giggling streams skip along,
With rocks that hum a silly song.
Every nook brings pure delight,
As joy dances, day and night.

Playful Shadows and Friendly Spirits

In the dappled light they dance,
A jolly band that loves to prance.
With every giggle, leaves do sway,
As whispers tease the bright'ning day.

Beneath the trees, the shadows play,
Tickling toes in a merry ballet.
Laughter echoes through the glen,
Where mischief blooms once and again.

They swap their hats and trade their shoes,
Bursting forth with silly news.
Like kittens chasing after dreams,
They spin in joyous, wild extremes.

Serenade of Silly Sounds

A trumpet blast from bubblegum,
As silly songs make all hearts hum.
Resounding hoots and honks delight,
In patches where the sun is bright.

The trees join in with rustling cheer,
A chorus loud for all to hear.
Each branch a note, each leaf a rhyme,
Creating magic, laughter, time.

When crickets chirp their evening tune,
The fireflies dance beneath the moon.
A serenade of pure delight,
With every chuckle, hearts feel light.

Chronicles of the Chuckling Forest

In winding paths where secrets lie,
The giggles soar up to the sky.
Every twig a tale to tell,
Where tickling winds weave laughter well.

Mischievous squirrels plot their pranks,
While playful frogs leap from their banks.
Each footfall drums a rhythm sweet,
As joy and whimsy warmly greet.

With painted rocks and silly signs,
The forest dances, twists, and twines.
In every nook, a spark of fun,
For all who wander 'neath the sun.

Golden Days of Grins

When daylight spills with golden rays,
And laughter fills the sunny ways.
The sunbeam's tickle on our nose,
Sparks joy that only friendship knows.

In fields of flowers, bright and bold,
Where secrets thrive and tales unfold.
Every smile a petal's kiss,
In this bright realm of perfect bliss.

With baskets filled with playful schemes,
We chase the clouds, we dance with dreams.
Those golden days, a treasure trove,
In every heart, their joy will rove.

Laughter's Secret Refuge

In a nook where chuckles bloom,
Silly shadows dance and zoom.
A band of frogs in tiny hats,
Joking with the nearby cats.

Bouncing bunnies, giggling loud,
Playing games beneath the cloud.
Each tickle from the grass below,
Makes the smiles just overflow.

Whispers of joy float on the breeze,
Carried by the playful trees.
Here, the silly meets the sweet,
Where laughter's heart is sure to beat.

With every joke and merry prank,
The air is filled, a joyful tank.
This haven of jest, our hidden place,
Where smiles grow and worries erase.

The Treetop Tavern of Delight

High above on branches wide,
Chirpy birds with gleeful pride.
Swinging from their leafy seats,
Sharing jokes with buzzing beats.

Squirrels juggle acorns round,
Their laughter echoes from the ground.
The wise old owl hoots with glee,
Mixing tales of joy so free.

Charming breezes, playful sighs,
Underneath the bright blue skies.
Each frolic spills like lemonade,
In this tavern none can fade.

Friendship beams like sunshine's ray,
Where silly thoughts come out to play.
In this spot where laughter thrives,
Heartfelt joy forever strives.

Mischievous Mirth in the Meadow

In a field where daisies sway,
Tiny creatures laugh and play.
A mouse in shoes, a duck in socks,
Telling tales from secret rocks.

Clouds join in, with forms so weird,
Just like dreams, imagination steered.
Giggling grasshoppers leap and glide,
Spreading joy far and wide.

Tickling winds make flowers shake,
Chortles rise, like ripples break.
In this patch of fun and cheer,
Silly secrets whisper near.

With every bounce and little cheer,
This daily joy we hold so dear.
Where mischief reigns and kindness flows,
A meadow full of whimsy grows.

The Quirky Clearing

In a spot where oddballs roam,
A patch of whimsy feels like home.
Rubber chickens dance with flair,
While trees sport hats beyond compare.

Laughter floats like dandelion seeds,
In this clearing, joy's the creed.
With each giggle, moods ignite,
Filling hearts with pure delight.

Silly shadows twist and prance,
Inviting everyone to dance.
Blissful moments intertwine,
In this space, where laughs align.

Here, the world seems soft and bright,
As funny antics fill the night.
A quirky place where we all meet,
And forge memories, oh so sweet.

Serenade of Silly

In a world where antics thrive,
Laughter echoes, spirits dive,
Jesters leap and clowns parade,
Every chuckle, a grand charade.

Bouncing balls and wobbly pies,
Funny faces, comical cries,
With every jump, a giggle flows,
Life's a circus, and joy grows.

Merry Moments

Whimsical hats and mismatched shoes,
Tangled tales, endless views,
Painted smiles on every cheek,
Moments spark, we laugh and peek.

Tickling toes on soft green grass,
Funny flips as the children pass,
Joyful shouts fill up the air,
In this place, we haven't a care.

Dance of Delight

Wiggly worms and froggy jumps,
Silly dances, playful bumps,
In this rhythm, laughter sways,
Each step brings smiles and sunny rays.

A twirl of skirts, a jig of glee,
The world joins in, oh so carefree,
With every whirl, the woes take flight,
Dancing shadows in the twilight.

Glee in the Grove

Hopping bunnies, dancing trees,
Whispers of joy in the gentle breeze,
Squirrelly tricks and giggly pranks,
Nature's laughter, its joyful flanks.

Butterflies flutter, bright and bold,
Silly stories that never get old,
Bubbles rising, bursting bright,
A canvas of laughter, pure delight.

Laughter's Meadow

In fields where chuckles sway and spin,
Bright flowers bloom with every grin,
A breeze of joy, it tickles ears,
As silly tales dissolve our fears.

A puppet troupe with nimble feet,
Dance to the rhythm of laughter sweet,
Witty words like bubbles rise,
In this bright world, we share our sighs.

The sun's a jester in the sky,
As butterflies begin to fly,
Each flutter brings a giggling sound,
In this joyful place, we're glory-bound.

Here, happiness is free and wild,
Every heart feels like a child,
With every step, the fun expands,
Together, let's make silly plans.

Whispering Happiness

In secret nooks where giggles bloom,
Joyful whispers chase away the gloom,
A ticklish tickle, a playful tease,
In every corner, laughter's breeze.

The trees are clowns with branches spread,
As shadows dance, no tears to shed,
A friendly breeze, it nudges all,
In this laughter, we feel so tall.

Bubbles rise with gleeful cheer,
Floating dreams, we hold so dear,
A symphony of light and sound,
Adventures in joy are always found.

With every puff and pitter-pat,
We share our secrets, oh, just like that,
In laughter's arms, we find our peace,
The sweetness of joy will never cease.

Joyful Echoes

In every chuckle, there's a spark,
A bouncing ball with every lark,
We skip and hop on sunshine beams,
In playful realms of giggling dreams.

Echoes swirl like melodies,

Running wild like stories told,
With every laugh, the world's our stage,
In these moments, we disengage.

Rabbits wear their silly hats,
While dancing round with friendly bats,
A carnival of sounds we make,
In this madness, joy won't break.

Let's chase the echoes, jump and play,
In shiny bliss, we'll spend our day,
For laughter's song is always near,
In joyful beats, we've naught to fear.

The Playground of Smiles

On slides of giggles, we all race,
With merry hearts, we find our place,
Each swinging laugh, a soaring flight,
With every spin, there's pure delight.

The merry-go-round sings to the sun,
Twirling tales of endless fun,
As eyes alight with wondrous glee,
In this playground, we are carefree.

A bounce, a leap, a new surprise,
Silly faces, sparkly eyes,
With playful shouts that fill the air,
We find our joy, we have our share.

Together here, we learn to share,
The laughter floats—beyond compare,
In this joyful space, let's all unite,
With every smile, the world feels right.

Fables in a Laughing Landscape

In a field where chuckles bloom,
The daisies dance, dispelling gloom.
Bumblebees buzz with silly tunes,
As rabbits bounce beneath the moons.

A frog in trousers leaps so high,
Trying to touch the sunny sky.
Squirrels play with acorn balls,
Sending giggles through the halls.

A turtle wears a hat so grand,
Strutting like a marching band.
With every step, a joyful sound,
In this land where laughs abound.

So come and join the playful spree,
Where laughter flows like a bright sea.
In this realm of mirth and cheer,
Whispers of joy are always near.

A Tangle of Ticklish Tales

In a forest full of smiles and glee,
Trees hold secrets, giggled with glee.
The owls hoot in a happy way,
Tickling the night until the day.

A monkey swings with silly flair,
Telling jokes without a care.
His friends, the birds, sing out in laughter,
Creating joy that echoes after.

A bear who juggles honey jars,
Falling clumsily, beneath the stars.
The ants parade in tiny shoes,
Marching to their own funny blues.

With each tale spun under the sun,
Laughter dances, as hearts run.
In this tangle of jokes and play,
Joyful spirits are here to stay.

The Joyful Lapse

In a world where pranks do thrive,
Among the giggles, spirits dive.
Silly creatures, bright and bold,
Sharing stories yet untold.

A parrot screams in silly tones,
Scaring cats and breaking bones.
The raccoons laugh with glee and fun,
As they steal snacks from everyone.

Clouds drift by like fluffy dreams,
Sprinkling joy in funny streams.
Every stumble, every slip,
Sends everyone into a trip.

So gather round, let laughter flow,
Feel the joy, let troubles go.
In the lapse of time, we find,
Silly moments, one of a kind.

The Lighthearted Retreat

In a nook where jests reside,
Laughter echoes, no need to hide.
Bubbles rise from every seam,
Dreams take flight, just like a dream.

A fish adorned with striped attire,
Swims and spins, a laugh inspired.
While hedgehogs play peek-a-boo,
Cuddly jokes from me to you.

A dandelion tickles the nose,
Making everyone laugh, who knows?
With joyful spirits swirling high,
Our hearts dance beneath the sky.

At this retreat of giggles and fun,
Together we shine like the sun.
With laughter as our guiding light,
Every moment feels just right.

The Perky Patch

In a place where laughter grows,
Tickling toes in silly rows.
Bouncing bunnies hop and play,
Chasing giggles through the day.

Giggles mingle with the breeze,
Like buzzing bees in laughter's tease.
A squirrel dons a jester's hat,
Poking fun at this and that.

Bright balloons float high in air,
Crafting joy without a care.
Frogs croak tunes of pure delight,
Under stars that twinkle bright.

Here all troubles seem to fade,
In this patch, no need for shade.
With every chuckle, hearts unite,
In a dance of pure delight.

Bashful Boughs and Buffoonery

Beneath the branches, whispers play,
Jokes are spun like wisps of hay.
A raccoon juggles shiny things,
While the owl hoots and laughter rings.

The saplings sway, they cannot hide,
As playful squirrels dart and glide.
With every wiggle, giggles rise,
Echoing back from friendly skies.

Tricks and pranks are all around,
As blossoms bloom from silly ground.
A turtle in a funny suit,
Struts his stuff, showing off his loot.

In this nook of cheeky glee,
Joy spreads wide, just like a spree.
And with each laugh, the world turns bright,
Crafting memories, pure delight.

Meadow of Merry Milestones

Sunlight spills on grassy beds,
Where laughter dances on our heads.
A puppy rolls in flowers bright,
Chasing shadows with delight.

Each step brings a cheeky grin,
As butterflies join in the spin.
Footprints small in muddy trails,
Marking joy where laughter sails.

Little hands throw daisies wide,
While giggles sway like the tide.
A snail slides past in silly grace,
With a comical, slow-moving pace.

The chalk-drawn games on pavement stay,
Circles of fun in bright display.
In this place where smiles abound,
Every moment is joy profound.

The Happy Haven

In a nook where sunshine beams,
Every giggle flows like streams.
With cheeky raccoons at the gate,
No trouble here, just laugh and skate.

A dragonfly, dressed in style,
Buzzing close, makes us all smile.
With tangled hair and muddy shoes,
We leap in puddles, nothing to lose.

Clouds above are cotton candy,
Dancing with a tune quite dandy.
A goat pranks the sheep with a leap,
In this haven, joy runs deep.

As shadows grow and day turns night,
Fireflies twinkle, a lovely sight.
In this place where fun won't cease,
We find our rhythm, purest peace.

Soiree of Whimsical Whispers

In a realm of playful cheer,
Where secrets dance upon the ear,
Bubbles float, and giggles bubble,
Every step ignites the trouble.

Jesters twirl with hats so bright,
Underneath the twinkling light,
Each chuckle lifts a vibrant song,
In this place, we all belong.

Silly games and laughter shared,
With a wink, no one is scared,
Hop and skip, let joy ignite,
As whispers weave through day and night.

So let the merry moments flow,
With every grin, our spirits grow,
For here we treasure laughter's gift,
In a world where shadows shift.

Treasures of the Ticklish Thicket

Among the trees where mischief hides,
A ticklish breeze, where joy abides,
Laughter spills from every nook,
In the stories that we cook.

Squirrels dance on tiny toes,
While giggles echo soft like prose,
Each corner holds a playful tease,
Among the twists of the playful trees.

With every step, the tickles bloom,
Creating smiles that chase the gloom,
From silly pranks to jests and fun,
In this thicket, joy's never done.

So gather forth, let laughter ring,
In this haven, let voices sing,
For treasures found in every laugh,
Are the moments that we craft.

The Jester's Boulevard

Down the path where giggles glide,
A jolly jester takes his stride,
With oversized shoes that squeak and squeal,
He spins a tale, oh what a deal!

Red noses bounce and smiles ignite,
As jests are shared in pure delight,
Every twist and turn, a jig,
In a world where joy is big.

Balloons drift up to pinky skies,
With candy dreams that mesmerize,
Follow the trail of silly sounds,
Where every chuckle knows no bounds.

So grab your friends and skip along,
In a pace to the happy song,
In this boulevard of fun and cheer,
Laughter whispers, come near, come near!

Where Laughter Lingers Long

In a sunlit spot where joy does sway,
Laughter lingers throughout the day,
With friendly faces and smiles wide,
Here, happiness can't be denied.

Witty remarks float on the breeze,
Twirling around like buzzing bees,
With every giggle, spirits rise,
A carousel of sweet surprise.

Tickle fights and pranks galore,
Fun surprises behind each door,
In every nook, a playful jest,
Laughter lingers, it's truly the best.

So join the fun, let worries cease,
In this realm of endless peace,
For in this place, we find our song,
Where laughter lingers, where we belong.

Echoes of Exultation

In the hollow of laughter, shadows dance,
With pranks and jests, they take their chance.
A whoopee cushion on the old oak seat,
Where giggles collide, and mischief is sweet.

Bubbles are floating in silly parade,
As squirrels in bowties join the charade.
Jokes tumble down like leaves in the breeze,
Each chuckle hangs heavy like honeyed teas.

The rabbits all tumble, in wild escapade,
With tickles and tumbles, their antics well-played.
A chorus of chuckles, soft as a sigh,
In this joyful realm, no one asks why.

Under the moonlight, the laughter takes flight,
With silly serenades lasting all night.
Echoes of joy, in the trees, they reside,
A symphony of fun, where giggles abide.

Sanctuary of Silliness

Here in this haven where whimsy is queen,
The grass is a carpet, the trees are a screen.
A cat wearing glasses, perched on a fence,
Is pondering life with sublime, silly sense.

The cake on the table is wobbling fast,
With sprinkles and giggles, a birthday blast.
Clowns with balloons frolic and prance,
In a world where each oddity gets a chance.

The tickle-bug army marches along,
With feathers in hand, they sing a bright song.
All creatures aligned for a festival's fight,
To see who can laugh at the silliest sight.

Light-hearted whispers among the tall blooms,
While daisies exchange their sweet, hearty plumes.
In this sanctuary, where laughter ignites,
Silliness reigns in the starry delights.

Blissful Breezes of the Bold

Through the pines, a breeze brings joyous cheer,
A laughing parade struts, with no hint of fear.
A dog in a tutu twirls with delight,
As sunbeams chuckle, embracing the sight.

The hedgehogs debate in a topsy-turvy way,
No need for decorum, just fun on display.
They roll in the grass, making hearts jump,
Creating a ruckus, a silly, sweet thump.

Giggles take flight on the wings of a kite,
As mischievous squirrels craft cackles of light.
A nutshell car zooms 'round a pretend track,
With drivers in pajamas, let's never look back.

Each breeze is a giggle, so fresh, so bold,
In this lush realm where silly tricks unfold.
The world fades away with laughter's warm embrace,
In blissful breezes, joy finds its place.

Glimmers of Delightful Chaos

In the heart of the forest, where shadows do creep,
A raucous assembly, no time for sleep.
The owls wear their hats, and the mice paint their toes,
In this joyous hubbub, anything goes.

A monkey on stilts wobbles with grace,
While rabbits play tag in a wild, mad race.
With confetti clouds that rain down with glee,
Every glance finds a grin, as funny as can be.

The pitter-patter feet join a dance so absurd,
Missteps turn magic, in laughter, they're stirred.
From gurgling brooks, sweet bubbles arise,
Glimmers of chaos light up the skies.

Cheerful pandemonium, life is a jest,
With pranks in the air, it's a curious fest.
In this realm of whimsy, hearts freely toss,
As joy weaves through moments, and chaos is gloss.

Meadow of Merrymaking Moments

In a field where jesters play,
Laughter bounces bright and gay,
Butterflies dance with flapping wings,
While squirrels mimic silly things.

The daisies chuckle, flowers sway,
As sunbeams join the fun-filled fray,
Breezes hum a playful song,
Inviting all to sing along.

A picnic spread with snacks galore,
Ants march in for a tasty score,
With fruit and giggles piled so high,
They munch on pies as they comply.

In this spot where joy ignites,
Every heart finds pure delights,
With every chuckle intertwined,
Merriment is redefined.

Fantasy of Frolicsome Foliage

Amidst the trees where shadows play,
Leaves whisper jokes and shout hooray,
A laughing brook splashes about,
Tickling toes, it bubbles out.

Fluffy clouds drift in a race,
As squirrels wear a silly face,
Frogs hop on to share their rhymes,
In this land of joyful times.

Giggling grasses sway with glee,
Nature's choir, one big spree,
The sunbeams tease the cool, soft shade,
Bright smiles flourish, never fade.

In this vivid, vibrant zone,
Every seed of laughter's sown,
What a dream, a funny scheme,
Where hilarity's the theme!

The Cheerful Canopy

Underneath a bright blue sky,
Birds perform their acrobats high,
Jokes are hidden in the breeze,
While playful antics tease the trees.

Merry blossoms burst with cheer,
Their sweet perfume draws friends near,
A picnic blanket lies askew,
And laughter buzzes like a brew.

Gnomes and fairies join the fun,
In a race that's just begun,
With splashes from a tiny stream,
They swirl and twirl in sunny dreams.

Happiness hangs from every bough,
As giggles echo, here and now,
A place where whimsy finds a way,
To brighten up the dullest day.

The Hideaway of Hearty Laughter

In a nook where chuckles bloom,
Joyful echoes chase the gloom,
Twinkling fireflies share their glow,
As nighttime giggles start to flow.

Rabbits host a daring race,
While owls hoot with silly grace,
Each whisper shared, a secret smile,
Where whimsy wanders for a while.

Toads croak jokes by the pond's edge,
While crickets dance upon a ledge,
A whimsical world, a laugh parade,
In this place where dreams are made.

Every heart is light and free,
Filled with fun and harmony,
In this hideaway, all year long,
Together here, we all belong.

Enchanted Exuberance

In a garden where laughter plays,
Flowers dance in sunny rays.
Bumblebees wear tiny hats,
Tickling cheeks of chubby rats.

A tree with a giggle, sways and bends,
Telling jokes to all its friends.
Bubbles pop, a chorus sings,
Oh, the joy that friendship brings!

Gnomes prance under moonlit skies,
Winking with mischievous eyes.
They juggle acorns, spin and twirl,
In this whimsical, wondrous world.

Sprinkles of joy in every nook,
A playful vibe in every crook.
With every chuckle, echoes grow,
Here, the heart's pure laughter flows.

Jolly Jaunt

Step into the land of cheer,
Where laughter is the only sphere.
Kites fly high, in giggly loops,
While squirrels join in silly scoops.

Buckets filled with jolly naps,
Ticklish toes and playful chaps.
Skip along the rocky path,
Follow the sounds of joyful wrath.

Rainbows here are made of dreams,
Sprinkling joy like playful beams.
Dancing shadows, bright confetti,
In this land, we all feel ready.

Laughter bubbles from each flower,
Filling hearts with playful power.
All around, a merry dance,
In this land, we take a chance.

Sunbeam Shenanigans

Sunbeams tumble, spin, and fall,
In this place, we find them all.
Butterflies with funny faces,
Lead us to the wildest places.

Chasing shadows, goofy grins,
Every moment, laughter wins.
Twinkling stars in daytime skies,
Winking down with joyful sighs.

Skip along the grassy lane,
Where silly antics rule the game.
A parade of frogs in coats,
With flapping wings and silly throats.

Every giggle, a sprinkle bright,
Transforms the day into pure light.
Join the fun, don't hesitate,
In this realm, we celebrate!

Elysian Echoes

In the land where fun takes flight,
Echoes giggle through the night.
Silly rabbits, hats askew,
Riding bicycles, just for two.

A picnic hosted by a fox,
Dancing with enchanted socks.
Toasting marshmallows made of cheer,
In this land, all laughs are near.

Wobbling geese sing silly tunes,
Floating high beneath the moons.
Whimsical thoughts in bubble chairs,
Where everyone is free from cares.

Tickles dance on sunlit beams,
As we drift through floating dreams.
In each corner, joy cascades,
A world alive with laughter's parades.

the Sanctuary of Smiles

In a haven where laughter blooms,
A ticklish breeze dispels the glooms.
Squirrels dance with acorn hats,
While butterflies tease playful chats.

Bubbles float on a sunbeam's trail,
Frogs croak jokes without fail.
Jolly gnomes in a merry line,
Sprinkle giggles like sweet sunshine.

Tickled trees sway to the sound,
Of chortles echoing all around.
Each shadow holds a giggling sprite,
Under clouds of fluffy delight.

So if you're feeling rather blue,
Set sail to where giggles brew.
For in this space, you'll surely find,
The happiest moments, intertwined.

Glimmers of Joyful Mischief

Chasing giggles in the breeze,
Where mischief dances with such ease.
Jumping over puddles wide,
With splashes echoing, side by side.

Whimsical wishes float above,
Crafting jokes made with pure love.
Rabbits fashion hats with flair,
While cheeky raccoons catch some air.

Stringing daisies in a row,
Spreading laughter wherever they go.
Fireflies twinkle, whisper secrets,
As the stars dance, no regrets.

In every corner, smiles ignite,
With pranks and puns that feel just right.
Let your troubles drift away,
In this realm where jesters play.

The Woodland of Whimsy

Where the trees wear funny grins,
And the brook hums cheerful sins.
Pixies playing tricks with flair,
Draping giggles in the air.

Wobbling mushrooms, strange and bright,
Encouraging a silly flight.
Bouncing bunnies in a race,
Bursting forth with giggly grace.

Paws of laughter on the ground,
In this space, joy can be found.
Jags of joy leap through the leaves,
Woven patterns love achieves.

So join the dance, let spirits free,
Share a joke under the tree.
In this woodland, mischief reigns,
Where each heart burst with happy gains.

Trails of Ticklish Delight

Winding paths where laughter flows,
In every nook, a giggle grows.
With every step, a chuckle near,
As nature whispers, 'Join the cheer!'

Silly squirrels with chatter quick,
Plan their antics, oh so slick.
Bouncing berries, ripe with fun,
As sunshine plays, we all become one.

Crickets chirp their merry tunes,
Underneath the smiling moons.
Each rustle holds a story bright,
In this realm of joyous light.

So follow the trail, let joy ignite,
With tickles and warmth, the heart feels light.
For on these paths, laughter thrives,
A treasure of joy, where kindness arrives.

Whimsical Ways in the Woods

In the forest, squirrels play,
Chasing shadows every day.
With acorns flying through the air,
Laughter echoes everywhere.

Frogs wear hats and jump around,
Their croaks create a silly sound.
Trees are draped in giggling vines,
While rabbit's dance on twisty lines.

Breezy whispers tell funny tales,
Of bunnies riding on the snails.
Mushrooms sprout with playful cheer,
As critters gather, far and near.

With every rustle, joy's alive,
In this woodland, we all thrive.
So let the whimsy run its course,
In this realm where laughter roars.

Lush Laughter of the Leafy Lane

Down the lane where daisies peek,
Cheerful faces play hide and seek.
Butterflies prance in sunny glow,
Creating smiles as they float and flow.

Stumbling on a playful shoe,
A monkey steals it just for you.
Giggling grass tickles your feet,
As clowns juggle fruits for a treat.

Breezes giggle through the trees,
Carrying chuckles on the knees.
Happy echoes from the brook,
Where fish wear glasses, take a look.

In this lane of endless fun,
Every moment is a run.
With laughter painted on the ground,
Joy is the only sound around.

Serene Shimmer of Smiling Skies

Balloons float in soft, sweet air,
They carry dreams without a care.
Clouds wear faces, bright and bold,
Telling secrets, tales untold.

Sunbeams dance on chubby cheeks,
As giggling children share their peaks.
Kites are flying, high and free,
Painting smiles for all to see.

In twilight hues of orange and pink,
Jokes are spinning, make you think.
Stars join in with twinkling glee,
As laughter floats from you to me.

So let the night begin to sing,
With silly tales on whispers' wing.
In the shimmer under the stars,
We find joy that's truly ours.

The Fruitful Fields of Frolic

In the meadows where we play,
Fruits are laughing every day.
Watermelons sing a tune,
As cherries dance beneath the moon.

Bouncing berries, round and bright,
Spin in circles, pure delight.
Apples giggle on the trees,
As butterflies sway on the breeze.

Harvest time is quite a scene,
With pumpkins grinning, oh so keen.
Laughter flows like rivers wide,
In these fields where fun won't hide.

So grab a friend, join the cheer,
In this land where joy is near.
With every skip and twirl we take,
Let's fill the world with laughter's wake.

The Frolicsome Refuge

In a land where laughter blooms,
Silly sounds break through the glooms.
Dancing shadows, cheerful prance,
Every creature shares a chance.

Bubbling brooks with giggles flow,
Ticklish breezes gently blow.
Bouncing balls of sunny cheer,
Joyful echoes, loud and clear.

Rusty old jokes and funny tricks,
Hide-and-seek with playful ticks.
Chasing tails and playful runs,
Smiles as bright as golden suns.

Underneath the starlit skies,
The moon makes silly faces rise.
In this place, the heart takes flight,
With laughter echoing through the night.

Harvest of Happines

Gathered here in playful throng,
Beneath the trees, we sing our song.
With baskets filled with giggles bright,
We share the joy from morn till night.

Fruits of laughter, ripe and sweet,
Every moment, pure and neat.
Jokes and jests we weave with care,
In this harvest, bliss to share.

Silly dances on the grass,
As time slips gently, gone too fast.
Tall tales told with winks and grins,
In this space, the fun begins.

When the sun dips, lanterns glow,
Twinkling lights begin to show.
Here in laughter's bounteous land,
We find the joy, hand in hand.

The Festive Fern Frond

Among the ferns that twist and sway,
　Fun abounds in bright display.
Tickles breeze through leafy bends,
　Laughter grows, it never ends.

Whimsical whispers in the air,
Garlands woven with flair to spare.
　Jumpy critters, full of zeal,
　In every corner, joy we feel.

Colorful hats atop our heads,
Bouncing back from silly dreads.
　In every giggle hides a song,
　In this place, we all belong.

As moonlight drapes the leafy shade,
　We dance and twirl, unafraid.
With every step and playful cheer,
　The festive spirit draws us near.

Mischievous Roots of Joy

In tangled roots, where secrets lie,
Mischief thrives, we dare to try.
Underfoot, a playful snare,
Finding laughter everywhere.

Puppy piles and chattering brooks,
Jumping frogs in silly looks.
In this spot, joy never tires,
With giddy giggles, heart desires.

Sticky fingers, muddy shoes,
In this fun, we cannot lose.
Every step, a new surprise,
With mischievous glints in our eyes.

At dusk, we share our tales out loud,
Proudly standing, heads unbowed.
In roots where laughter springs anew,
We weave a world, just me and you.

A Symphony of Snickers

Laughter dances in the breeze,
As ticklish whispers float with ease.
Bouncing gnomes on pogo sticks,
Playful pranks and funny tricks.

Juggling squirrels, nuts in hand,
Twirling around, oh isn't it grand?
A chorus of chuckles fills the air,
Joyful notes without a care.

Frolicking frogs in silly hats,
Doing the cha-cha with chubby cats.
The air is sweet with jokes and jests,
Where hearty laughter never rests.

In this lively, carefree place,
Every smile wears a bright trace.
With every giggle, hearts take flight,
In this symphony of delight.

Where Joy Springs Eternal

Tiny turtles on roller skates,
Turn frowns into merry traits.
Joy bubbles up like fizzy soda,
Chasing gloom like a playfuloda.

Bouncing bunnies, bright and bold,
Sharing secrets never told.
Sunshine spills like liquid gold,
In a place where warmth unfolds.

Giggles sprout from every seed,
Mixing laughter with a good deed.
Where showers of smiles fall like rain,
And happiness is never plain.

Happy faces, shiny and round,
In this haven, joy is found.
In playful prances, troubles flee,
A world where everyone laughs with glee.

The Garden of Happy Whispers

Breezy breezes play and sway,
Tickling ears with things to say.
Witty wands with riddle mints,
Crafting laughs in playful hints.

Silly squirrels in tiny boots,
Dance around with goofy hoots.
Chasing shadows under trees,
Where laughter floats upon the breeze.

Where sunbeams bounce like children free,
Every giggle sings like a sea.
Whispers filled with pure delight,
Brighten up the day and night.

In this garden, joy won't cease,
Woven tightly into peace.
A symphony of glee and cheer,
A space where happiness draws near.

Festive Footfalls in the Ferns

Silly shadows shift and sway,
As laughter leads the merry way.
Frogs in tuxedos croon with flair,
Dancing feet with extra care.

Swaying vines whisper secret jokes,
Even the flowers chuckle and poke.
With every step, there's glee beneath,
On a path of joy and wreath.

Around the bend, a giggling brook,
Hums sweet tunes in every nook.
Where footfalls beat a happy tune,
And smiles blossom like flowers in June.

In this festival of mirth and cheer,
Brightened hearts gather near.
With each fond chuckle, spirits rise,
In this joyous dance, laughter flies.

Rhapsody of Raucous Laughter

In a place where jests bloom bright,
Laughter dances, taking flight.
Tickling toes and silly faces,
Joyful echoes fill the spaces.

Bouncing balls and prancing feet,
Seriousness is on the street.
With every chuckle, skies grow clear,
All worries vanish, lost in cheer.

Whimsical creatures play a tune,
Underneath the watchful moon.
Jokes tumble out like leaves in fall,
A symphony of gaiety for all.

When the sun sets, giggles swell,
In a tale that we all can tell.
So come along, join the spree,
In this realm of jubilee.

Mirth's Secret Haven

Where the daisies wear a grin,
And the breezes pull you in.
Riddles dance upon the air,
Giggling fairies everywhere.

A twist of fate, a silly sight,
Laughter springs like morning light.
Chasing shadows of old frowns,
Here, we swap our dreary crowns.

With playful pranks that spin and twirl,
The happiest of dreams unfurl.
Tripping over, rolling down,
Each moment met with joy, not frowns.

Ticklish whispers fill the trees,
Sprinkling smiles like golden leaves.
Join the dance, let worries flee,
In this nook of jubilee.

Radiant Riddles

Underneath a sunlit haze,
Laughter simmers, sets ablaze.
Jiggly sprites weave tales so sweet,
In verses filled with playful beat.

Twisted words and dreary sounds,
Here they vanish, joy abounds.
Riddles tumble, round and round,
In this laughter, joy is found.

Picture this—a hopping hare,
Dancing lightly through the air.
Chickens play a game of tag,
While grumpy clouds begin to wag.

But as day begins to wane,
Silliness shall not remain,
As night descends, the mirth takes flight,
Awakening the stars so bright.

Tickled Twilights

In dusky hours, giggles creep,
Painting skies as dreamers leap.
With every chuckle, night awakes,
And whispering wind skips through the lakes.

A squirrel dons a coat of stripes,
While owls share their nibbled bites.
Mirthful dances on the green,
In the twilight, laughter's seen.

Carts of candy, sweet delight,
Flying high with stars so bright.
Bouncing jokes across the glen,
Who could count to ten again?

When darkness falls, the fun expands,
With silly shadows, hand in hands.
So gather 'round, let giggles stir,
In this realm where laughter purrs.

Chuckles Under the Canopy

Beneath the leaves, laughter spills,
Silly critters dance on hills.
With squeaks and squeals, they frolic round,
In this merry spot, joy is found.

A whispering breeze, a tickling touch,
A squirrel tells tales that make us clutch
Our bellies tight, as we double up,
For fun always fills this never-ending cup.

The sun peeks through, a playful friend,
As shadows bounce and twist, they bend.
Jumping jests and gleeful pranks,
In this whimsical world, all give thanks.

Oh, the giggles that weave through the air,
Every chuckle hugs without a care.
With every bound, every joyful ring,
Life's simple pleasures make our hearts sing.

Frolicsome Fables

A rabbit raced with floppy ears,
Telling tales that tickle fears.
He spun a yarn of pie and cake,
As everyone gasped—a giant snake!

The turtle laughed, "That's truly bold!"
With his slow smile, a sight to behold.
He spun his fable of sweet delight,
As fruit trees danced in the moonlight.

Mischief-makers in the tall grass,
Playing pranks that make moments pass.
A blanket of giggles spreads so wide,
In every nook, joy can't hide.

Adventures bloom, far and near,
With every whimsy, there's naught to fear.
The laughter grows until it flows,
In frolicsome fables, the humor glows.

The Joyful Oasis

In a world where smiles bubble up,
Where clouds of fluff fill every cup.
With sprinkles of laughter all around,
In this joyful oasis, bliss is found.

The sun dangles low, with rays so bright,
While creatures join a comical fight.
A duck wears socks, a hat askew,
In every moment, something new.

Picnics unfold on soft green grass,
As ants perform their little dance.
Sandwiches giggle, and fruit takes flight,
In this haven of joy, all feels right.

Together we laugh, together we play,
In this playful paradise, we'll stay.
Every chuckle, every gleam,
Unfolds the magic of a dream.

Grinning Shadows

When daylight wanes and shadows creep,
Secrets of laughter we all will keep.
Beneath the moonlight, gleeful sights,
With grinning shadows, we ignite nights.

The fireflies flicker, twinkling bright,
Their dance invites us to delight.
Silly stories from trees so tall,
Echo along, laughter's call.

We sneak a peek, a giggly stare,
As woodland critters have no care.
They tumble and roll, a joyful spree,
In these shaded realms, we feel so free.

With every chuckle, we become entwined,
In the comfort of joy, our hearts aligned.
So let us play, let our spirits soar,
With grinning shadows, forevermore.

Cheery Companions

In a place where laughter's loud,
Friends gather, forming a crowd.
With silly hats and shoes too big,
They dance around, each doing a jig.

Jokes fly like butterflies bright,
Tickling ribs, a joyful sight.
With every giggle, spirits soar,
In this merry land, there's always more.

Ticklish slaps and playful shoves,
Bound by laughter, the best of loves.
In every corner, gleeful sounds,
Happiness in all bounds.

Together they chase the frowns away,
Turning gloom into a bright play.
With pranks and puns, the mischief brews,
They spread their joy like morning hues.

Blissful Breeze

A whisper floats on the sunny air,
With giggles hidden everywhere.
Laughter dances in the trees,
Mischief carried on the breeze.

Clouds of fluff, laughter rolls fast,
Every heart feeling unsurpassed.
A slip, a trip, a pie takes flight,
In this wild and silly delight.

Chasing each other, round and round,
As joy creates a joyful sound.
They tumble and spin without a care,
Painting smiles that linger in the air.

Silly songs on a warm spring day,
With melodies that twist and sway.
In the breeze, the laughter's king,
In every moment, joy they bring.

Heartfelt Hilarity

Beneath the sun, where smiles abound,
Comedic moments spin around.
A fumble here, a giggle there,
With funny faces, an endless affair.

In perfect sync, their jokes collide,
Their humor an unstoppable tide.
As raucous laughter fills the space,
Each hearty chuckle leaves a trace.

Like squirrels who dance in silly shoes,
Crafting laughter with playful cues.
In every jest, a loving touch,
Their heartfelt humor means so much.

Until the stars peek in the night,
They share their joy, a pure delight.
With endless stories shared with cheer,
Their hearts entwined, forever near.

Charmed Chuckles

A gathering of friends so dear,
With jokes that sparkle, bright and clear.
Giddy giggles collide in the air,
Each one radiating joyous flair.

With wobbly chairs and playful quirks,
Silly games and zany perks.
A buzzing hum of laughter grows,
As playful banter surely flows.

Twirling tales of comical fates,
With jesters jumping on tiny plates.
In this realm where smiles appear,
laughter echoing, sweet and sincere.

Through every glance, a shared delight,
They spin in circles, hearts so light.
In heaven of humor, friends unite,
Creating mirth, a pure delight.

Hallowed Hideaway of Laughter

In a nook where chuckles bloom,
Ticklish whispers fill the room.
Bouncing jokes like rubber balls,
Every giggle gently calls.

Jumping beans and funny hats,
Silly faces, playful chats.
A jiggle here, a wiggle there,
In this spot, we shed our care.

The Thicket of Tickling Thoughts

A forest made of silly dreams,
With wobbly walks and wiggly schemes.
Tickles hide behind each tree,
Come explore, just you and me.

Feathers float on breezy air,
Laughter dances everywhere.
A tickle fight, a game of chase,
In this thicket, joy we embrace.

Joyous Journeys and Silly Stories

On a path where giggles roam,
Every turn feels just like home.
Silly tales that twist and play,
Brighten up the dullest day.

Wobbling wonders leap about,
In this land, there's never doubt.
With every step, our hearts take flight,
Chasing laughter, pure delight.

The Exuberant Hideout

A secret spot where smiles grow wide,
With zany antics, joy won't hide.
Jolly songs and funny games,
In this hideout, none feels shame.

Whirling giggles swirl like air,
Giddy hearts shed every care.
Surrounded by our laughter's sound,
In this place, pure fun is found.

Rays of Radiant Revelry

In the bright field where giggles play,
Silly shadows come out to sway.
Laughter dances on the breeze,
Tickled petals sway with ease.

Jesters prance in polka dots,
Chasing squirrels in funny trots.
Every corner bursts with cheer,
Whispers of joy fill the sphere.

The Grove of Gleeful Hearts

Amidst the trees, the chuckles flow,
Bouncing bugs put on a show.
Flowers chuckle, breezes sigh,
Caught in laughter, time slips by.

Giggling brook sings a tune,
Merriment beneath the moon.
Bouncing bunnies join the fun,
Underneath the golden sun.

Enchanted Laughter Land

Where spritelike whispers tickle the air,
Merry fairies dance without a care.
Rainbows flip and flit with glee,
Joyful echoes—just let them be.

Witty winks from every flower,
Humor blooms in every hour.
Twirling petals, laughter spins,
Magic lives where fun begins.

Dappled Sunlight and Glee

Bouncing beams of light so bright,
Giggles hide in plain sight.
A parade of chuckles, joyous and free,
Sprinting shadows, come join me!

Whimsical winds play tricks on leaves,
Laughter weaves through the eaves.
A jolly riddle wraps the day,
In this fun-filled, vibrant sway.

Vibrant Visions of Joy.

In fields where colors dance and sway,
A ticklish breeze comes out to play.
Jolly jests float on the air,
While giggles bloom like flowers rare.

Chasing shadows, silly and spry,
Bouncing like bubbles, oh so high.
Laughter leaps from tree to tree,
Painting smiles, wild and free.

A parade of whispers, silly and bright,
Riding the waves of morning light.
With every step, the humor flows,
In a joyful world, where the giggle grows.

Frogs don hats, and birds wear shoes,
Dancing in rhythm to the funny blues.
Echoes of joy, a sweet serenade,
In this land where laughter never fades.

Whispers in the Laughter Woods

In a wood where snickers bloom,
Breezes sweep away all gloom.
Leaves laugh and twist in glee,
A merry world, just let it be.

Squirrels juggling acorns high,
In the canopy, they fly by.
Witty whispers fill the breeze,
Tickling hearts with playful tease.

Bubbles sparkle, float, and burst,
Spreading giggles, a funny thirst.
Elves tell tales of prankster deeds,
Binding joy like magic beads.

Crickets chirp, a joyful tune,
Underneath the laughing moon.
In this realm, all feel alive,
Where humor and joy always thrive.

Secrets of the Jolly Grove

In a grove where secrets hide,
Curly giggles swell with pride.
Whimsical creatures stir the pot,
In a world where fun is caught.

With every rustle, chuckles sneak,
As hints of mirth begin to speak.
Bouncy bunnies, hats askew,
Churning laughter, fresh as dew.

Twists of fate in playful schemes,
Tickle the air like forgotten dreams.
Each twist and turn, a laugh unfurls,
In the heart of this wonder-world.

Mirthful whispers spin around,
Magic lies beneath the ground.
In this realm where joy runs wild,
Every heart is a laughing child.

Echoes of Hidden Chuckles

Beneath the trees, a titter rings,
As shadows dance with silly swings.
Whiskers twitch on a grinning fox,
Telling tales from the laughter box.

Chortles echo through the glen,
Frolicking fun begins again.
Ribbons of giggles spin and curl,
In a cheerful, magical whirl.

Bouncing birds on branches sway,
Make merry music bright as day.
Echoes of hilarity bounce forth,
Filling the air with joyous mirth.

In this place of whimsical cheer,
Laughter's melody rings so clear.
Every note a treasure found,
In a realm where silliness abounds.

The Meadow of Merriment

In a field where laughter grows,
Jumpy rabbits strike a pose.
Chasing shadows, oh what fun,
Tickled by the morning sun.

Butterflies dance with silly grace,
Making funny faces, a wild race.
Each flower giggles, petals bright,
As whispers of joy take flight.

Silly squirrels play peek-a-boo,
Wobble around on soft dewy dew.
With every leap, they bring delight,
Transforming day from dull to bright.

Under skies of giggly blue,
Chuckle softly, yes, it's true.
In this meadow, hearts are light,
Where laughter lingers, pure delight.

Beneath the Joyful Canopy

Underneath the trees so high,
Sings a bird with a funny cry.
Its melodies twist and twirl,
Spinning giggles in a whirl.

Swaying branches, dance along,
Echoing a soft, sweet song.
A squirrel squeaks, and all will laugh,
In this enchanted frolic path.

Sunbeams scatter, playful rays,
Tickling leaves in cheeky ways.
With every rustle, joy takes flight,
Painting smiles in sheer delight.

Under the arches green and wide,
Every creature comes to glide.
In dappled light, they'll dare to dream,
In this realm of laughter's beam.

Serendipity in Smiles

A roaming bear, a jolly sight,
Wears a hat that's far too tight.
He trips on roots, oh what a show,
Rolling over, in the glow!

A parrot cracks its best joke yet,
Leaving all who hear in fret.
With every squawk, the joy expands,
Filling hearts and warming hands.

Tiny ants in a conga line,
Marching 'round without a sign.
Their tiny feet tap-tap so sweet,
A tiny rhythm, a funny beat.

With laughter as the sweetest sound,
In each smile, joy can be found.
In every twirl and cheer and glance,
Life's a whimsical, joyful dance.

The Fable of Frolicking Friends

In a glen where laughter roams,
Bouncing buddies make their homes.
A hedgehog with a prickly hat,
Leads the way in a merry chat.

A rabbit spins, falls with a flop,
But quickly bounces, can't quite stop.
Jumping high, the joy ignites,
Under stars on playful nights.

Together they scheme, plan a prank,
Hiding pies near the old oak plank.
When fur and feathers finally meet,
Laughter echoes, life's a treat.

With tales of fun that never end,
Where even the shyest will blend.
In this fable, joy's the key,
With frolicking friends, wild and free.

Humming Harmony of Happiness

In fields where laughter reigns supreme,
The flowers sing a silly theme.
Bumblebees in bowties zoom,
Tickling daisies, bright with bloom.

A funny worm makes quite the show,
He wears a hat, a real-life pro.
With gentle giggles, all around,
Joy echoes softly, sweetly found.

Each quack and squeak creates a tune,
Dancing shadows spun by the moon.
To skip and hop, oh what delight,
In this vast space, all feels just right.

In every corner, spirits prance,
Inviting all to join the dance.
With silly songs and playful cheer,
This melody sings, forever near.

Cavern of Chuckling Crickets

In caverns deep, the crickets laugh,
Turning shadows into a cast.
With every chirp, a chuckle sounds,
Through twisty paths, joy abounds.

A funny bat in shades like night,
Flies in circles, what a sight!
He giggles with each swift descent,
In this cave, time is well spent.

Echoes bounce off stony walls,
As playful jesters make their calls.
A dance of flickers, bright and neat,
Jumbling giggles, a rhythmic beat.

With each tiny shout, the night feels bright,
In the merriment of pure delight.
The crickets' chorus, a merry team,
Filling the dark with laughter's gleam.

Dance of the Joyful Spirits

In twilight's glow, the spirits play,
Twisting, twirling till break of day.
With flapping wings, they swoop and dive,
Creating joy, oh how they thrive!

Their laughter floats like gentle mist,
Every flicker, a playful twist.
A waltz with trees in glowing light,
As shadows giggle in the night.

With each new step, a silly cheer,
The air bursts forth with laughter here.
The rhythm's caught by roots below,
In happy sway, together flow.

Spirits whisper funny tales,
Of merry journeys, joyful trails.
In this lightness, hearts take flight,
Dancing with glee till morning light.

Beneath the Boughs of Banter

Beneath the branches, tales unfold,
Of silly squirrels and secrets told.
With acorns tossed and laughter shared,
Every critter, joyfully paired.

Rabbits hop to a beat so bright,
Filling the air with pure delight.
A chorus formed of giggles sweet,
Beneath the shade, where moments meet.

A wise old owl, with glasses on,
Winks and hoots till the break of dawn.
His jests, a treasure for all to find,
In this bounteous spot, forever kind.

So gather close, let spirits soar,
In this realm of laughter, explore.
Under boughs where joy won't cease,
Every chuckle brings us peace.

Celestial Laughter

In skies where chuckles tumble down,
Stars wink with glee, a vibrant crown.
The moon plays tricks, a playful jest,
While comets dance in a jestful quest.

Puppies chase clouds, tails wagging high,
Cats join in, with a flutter and fly.
Each giggle bounces on the soft air,
Tickling the senses, laughter to share.

Trees wear hats of colorful hues,
With squirrels prancing in fancy shoes.
A tickle from winds, they scamper about,
Creating a whirl of joy and shout.

And as the day meanders to night,
The stars gather round for a laughter fight.
Under this dome of chortles and cheers,
We spin in circles, shedding our fears.

Festooned with Fun

Balloons float by like dreams in flight,
Colors clash in a joyful sight.
Laughter bubbles from every nook,
As butterflies dance with a cheerful hook.

Jokers play games, and giggles ensue,
Ticklish toes in the morning dew.
Silly hats and mismatched shoes,
Each step a stumble, each stumble a bruise.

Juggling clowns with pies in hand,
A whipped cream shower, oh what a stand!
The crowd erupts, such a playful scene,
Where humor reigns, and all is serene.

Amid the joy, a playful parade,
With laughter echoing, never to fade.
In this garden of merriment so grand,
Fun festoons the air, hand in hand.

The Clearing of Cheerful Whines

In a field where frowns turn to cheer,
Whispers of giggles fill the atmosphere.
Where daisies dance on a joyful spree,
And even the grumps can chuckle with glee.

Children skip with blossoms in tow,
Every step, a comedic show.
A rabbit hops, wearing a grin,
While the sun shines bright, inviting them in.

The breeze carries jokes that twist and shout,
As shadows leap and wander about.
Everyone joins in a playful embrace,
Finding delight in this whimsical space.

And as twilight paints the horizon wide,
Laughter breezes in like a joyful tide.
In this place where whines turn to sweeps,
The heart finds warmth while laughter leaps.

Where Giggling Breezes Blow

A melody soft, a bubbling brook,
Giggling breezes, come take a look.
The flowers sway in a rhythmic dance,
Inviting all for a playful chance.

The sun beams laughter at every hue,
As butterflies flutter, all bright and new.
Kites soar high, painting the sky,
With trails of chuckles that never die.

In corners of joy where whispers play,
Puppies tumble, their antics on display.
With every bark a punchline rings,
In this realm where the laughter sings.

And as shadows lengthen, the fun won't cease,
For here, every giggle is a piece of peace.
So come along, where chuckles flow,
In this realm where the breezes know.

www.ingramcontent.com/pod-product-compliance
Lightning Source LLC
Chambersburg PA
CBHW051651160426
43209CB00004B/881